MINDFUL ME
Exploring Emotions

Every emotion is an adventure ...

First published in Great Britain in 2018 by The Watts
Publishing Group

Copyright © The Watts Publishing Group, 2018

ISBN: 978 1 4451 5726 9 (hbk)
ISBN: 978 1 4451 5727 6 (pbk)

Managing editor: Victoria Brooker
Creative design: Lisa Peacock

Printed in China

Franklin Watts is a division of
Hachette Children's Books,
an Hachette UK company.
Carmelite House
50 Victoria Embankment
London EC4Y 0DZ

www.hachette.co.uk
www.franklinwatts.co.uk

MINDFUL ME
EXPLORING EMOTIONS

A Mindfulness Guide
to Dealing with Emotions

Written by
Paul Christelis

Illustrated by
Elisa Paganelli

W
FRANKLIN
WATTS

WHAT IS MINDFULNESS?

Mindfulness is a way of paying attention to our present
moment experience with an attitude of kindness and
curiosity. Most of the time, our attention is distracted – often
by thoughts about the past or future – and this can make us
feel jumpy, worried, self-critical and confused.

By gently moving our focus from our busy minds and into
the present moment (for example, by noticing sensations
and emotions in our bodies, without judging them or
wishing them to be different) we begin to let go of
distraction and learn to tap into the ever-present
supply of joy and ease that resides in each
moment. Mindfulness can also help us
to improve concentration, calm
unpleasant emotions, even boost
our immune systems.

In this book, children are gently guided into mindfulness exercises that encourage an exploration of emotions. By being curious about their 'inner weather' – accepting their current emotional experience rather than judging it – they begin to cultivate a healthy relationship with emotions. Rather than identifying themselves with the emotion they are feeling ("I am angry!") children begin to see that emotions are simply natural experiences that come and go ("Right now, I am feeling anger in my belly"). The benefits of making this shift are explored in the story.

The book can be read interactively, allowing readers to pause at various points and bring their attention to what they are noticing.
The **PAUSE BUTTON** in the text suggests where you might encourage readers to be curious about what's going on for them – in their minds, bodies, breathing, etc. Each time this **PAUSE BUTTON** is used, mindfulness is deepened. Don't rush this pause; really allow enough time for children to tune into their experience.

It doesn't matter if what they notice feels pleasant or unpleasant: what's important is to pay attention to it with a friendly attitude. This will introduce them to a way of being in the world that promotes health and happiness.

Everyone notices the **weather** outside, don't they?

Have a look now: is it sunny or cloudy?
Rainy or dry? Windy or calm? Or something else?

But did you realise that weather occurs inside you, too? In fact, if you take a look, you'll feel it right now. We call this inner weather **emotions**. And just like the weather outside, emotions are completely natural.

Today is Sports Day at school. The weather outside is warm
and sunny, but for many children it's very different.
Here's Abu; he's not feeling warm and sunny at all!

Inside, Abu is experiencing a different kind of weather. For him, running in a race makes him feel nervous. It's like watching a storm approaching: it can be scary.

And here's Sally, also about to run in the race. Her inner weather is different from Abu's. Can you tell what emotion she's experiencing?

Sally enjoys competing. She's feeling **excitement** and can't wait for the race to start.

How would you describe Sally's weather? When you are about to run in a race, what's your weather like?

PAUSE BUTTON

Over at the skipping race, Manisha has tripped on her rope just before the finish line. She's feeling really **angry** with herself. She could have won if she'd been more careful!

How could I be so stupid?!

Anger can feel like burning hot sun. When you feel angry, where in your body do you feel the burning? Your belly? Your head? Somewhere else?

PAUSE BUTTON

And this is Kenton. His ankle is fractured so he can't participate in any sport today. The **sadness** and disappointment he feels is like a grey, drizzly day that seems to last forever!

Tom is sitting close to Kenton but there are no rain clouds over him – he has just completed four events in a row, and now he's feeling **relief** (as well as some achy muscles!). For him, relief is like a cool breeze on a hot day.

Later in the day, the weather is changing … And guess what?
Just like the weather, the children's emotions are changing, too.

Abu was nervous, but now he's finished his race and is eating a big bowl of chocolate ice cream.

Can you tell what Abu is feeling now? When you eat something delicious, what feelings do you experience?

PAUSE BUTTON

Sally's excitement has changed, too. She won her race, but now she's at the hospital visiting her sick grandma. She feels a little sad.

Meanwhile, Manisha is no longer angry with herself. She was awarded a medal for perseverance and now she's feeling **proud**!

No more drizzle for Kenton! His cast has been removed and now he's feeling happy.

And Tom is back home now with nothing to do.
Relief has turned to **boredom**.

Changes in our inner weather happen all the time. It's natural and normal. Sometimes the weather feels pleasant; for example, when we feel happy, relieved or excited. And sometimes it feels unpleasant; when we feel anger, sadness or frustration.

The good news is, we don't have to worry about getting stuck with unpleasant emotions because these won't last forever! Perhaps you are feeling sad this morning, but this afternoon … who knows?!

We can't predict how we will feel later, and we can't always change our emotions while we are feeling them. But, we can learn to be with these emotions as we feel them. We accept them just as they are.

"I know you are here, Sadness. It's okay because I know you are just a feeling and you will pass …"

"Hello Nervous feeling in my belly! You feel uncomfortable but I know you won't stay long."

Take a moment to be with what you are feeling right now. How's your inner weather? Sunny? Gloomy? Stormy? Or perhaps there is not a lot going on and you don't feel very much – that's fine, too.

 **PAUSE BUTTON**

"Right now, I'm not feeling anything in particular, and that's perfectly fine."

Sometimes, when weather is very **stormy**, it feels as if you might get blown away by the strong winds. Anger or nervousness can feel like powerful storms!

When you're in a storm of emotions, try naming the emotion you are experiencing. When you name what you are feeling, the storm often calms down a little and doesn't feel so powerful.

"Here's that nervous feeling again."

"This is anger I'm feeling."

So take the time to check your personal weather report every day.

And remember that we all experience all kinds of weather.
Our friends, parents, teachers, pets … we all have sunny
moments, scary moments and not-feeling-very-much-at-all
moments.

HELLO, WEATHER!

HOW ARE YOU TODAY?

Enjoy the pleasant feelings when they are present, and
remember that the unpleasant ones will pass.

NOTES FOR PARENTS AND TEACHERS

Here are a few other mindfulness exercises and suggestions to add to your child's Mindful Toolkit. These are simple, effective, and above all, fun to do!

WEEKLY WEATHER PATTERNS

Find a place at home to display a Weekly Weather Chart. This might be on a bedroom wall, a fridge, or a notice board. You can have fun making one, including days of the week and times of the day: Morning; Afternoon; Evening. Each morning, ask your child to check his or her inner weather, and then place a coloured sticker corresponding to that emotion on the chart (for example, Blue = Sad; Yellow = Happy; Red = Angry). Do the same for the other times of day. At the end of the week, take down the chart and have a look at the weekly weather pattern. It's likely that there will be a variety of colours suggesting changing emotions. If there is a predominance of one colour, you can talk about this too: was it a particularly anxious week, or a sad one? Looking at the internal weather in this way allows children to notice that emotions constantly come and go. This makes difficult emotions easier to acknowledge and accept.

TAKE ACTION

Acknowledging difficult emotions can help to ease their intensity but it is also helpful to look at what is needed in that moment to ensure that the child feels safe and resourceful. A cuddle or a hug, perhaps? Or maybe calling to mind a fond memory or visualising a special place? It's important to notice that the intention of such action is not to avoid the child's feelings. Rather, the action comes from a place of fully accepting the child's experience and compassionately responding to it. This teaches children to 'self soothe' when the going feels rough. Essentially, you are saying: "You feel really sad right now, and that's okay, but also you know that you are safe and loved no matter what you feel."

MAGIC MINUTE

Scientific research shows that if we are able to observe the physical sensations of difficult emotions without getting caught up in our thoughts about them, then the chemical component of that emotion flushes itself out of our system, returning us to a state of relative ease. All it takes is a minute or two.

So when your child is in the grip of a strong emotion, suggest that she takes a Magic Minute to notice it: where in the body is the angry feeling? What happens when she pays attention to this feeling? Does it get stronger or softer? Does it move? Are other parts of the body affected? After timing a minute, if the emotion is still intense, take another 30 seconds. The intensity is likely to have waned. A minute can make all the difference! (N.B. It is also possible to take a minute to notice pleasant feelings, too!)

INVISIBLE RAINCOAT

Sometimes we can feel really battered by stormy emotions. When this happens, it's time to put on your Invisible Raincoat to protect you! If your child needs extra support, ask them to imagine their very own personal raincoat. What colour is it? Does it have a pattern or interesting design? What is it made of? When they're feeling blown away by a rainstorm of emotions, encourage them to slip into their raincoat. It won't stop the storm but it can protect them from getting soaked! Ask them to imagine the raindrops bouncing off the protective layer and patiently wait for the storm to pass.

SHARE THE WEATHER

Encourage children to notice that everyone – even parents, teachers, other adults, pets – experiences changing emotions. We are all in the same boat! Sometimes a parent might be feeling sadness or irritation and may also need some space and time to sit through this. You can assist young people to pay attention to this by openly acknowledging and sharing how you are feeling. The intention in sharing feelings is to create an inclusive space where it is possible to bring empathy and compassion to the relationship, without judging one another for feeling the way we do.

FURTHER READING

Acorns to Great Acorns: Meditations for Children, Marie Delanote
(Findhorn Press Ltd, 2017)

Glad to be Dan: Discover How Mindfulness Helps Dan to Be Happy Every Day,
Jo Howarth and Jude Lennon (CreateSpace Independent Publishing Platform, 2016)

Master of Mindfulness: How to be Your Own Superhero in Times of Stress, Laurie Grossman
(New Harbinger, 2016)

Mindful Monkey, Happy Panda, Lauren Alderfer and Kerry Lee McLean
(Wisdom Publications, 2011)

Mindful Movements: Ten Exercises for Well-being, Wietske Vriezen
(Parallax Press, 2008)

Planting Seeds: Practicing Mindfulness with Children, Thich Nhat Hanh
(Parallax Press, 2011)

Sitting Still Like a Frog, Eline Snel
(Shambhala Publications Inc., 2014)